About Skill Builders
Grammar
Grade 5

Welcome to Skill Builders *Grammar* for fifth grade. This book is designed to improve children's grammar skills through focused practice. This full-color workbook contains grade-level-appropriate activities based on national standards to help ensure that children master basic skills before progressing.

More than 70 pages of activities cover essential grammar skills, such as parts of speech, capitalization, punctuation, and usage. The book's colorful, inviting format, easy-to-follow directions, and clear examples help build children's confidence and make grammar more accessible and enjoyable.

The Skill Builders series offers workbooks that are perfect for keeping skills sharp during the school year or preparing children for the next grade.

Credits:
Content Editor: Ginny Swinson
Copy Editor: Beki Benning
Layout and Cover Design: Nick Greenwood

D1733519

carsondellosa.com
Carson-Dellosa Publishing, LLC
Greensboro, North Carolina

ISBN: 978-1-936023-22-6
05-025161151

Table of Contents

Common and Proper Nouns

Underline each common noun and circle each proper noun.

A **common noun** names a general person, place, thing, or idea.
A **proper noun** names a specific person, place, thing, or idea.

Example: (Emma) walked her dog to the park.

1. A gerbil is a mammal that is related to the hamster.

2. Many species of gerbil live in Asia and Africa.

3. Gerbils do not have many natural enemies.

4. Gerbils have strong hind legs that help them jump high and escape from birds and other predators.

5. Gerbils that are sold in pet stores today are descendants of gerbils captured in Mongolia decades earlier.

6. Christopher went to Pet Town to purchase a gerbil, some food, and a water bottle.

7. Christopher took his gerbil home to show his brother, Shane, and his sister, Sierra.

8. The family agreed that a gerbil is a cute and interesting pet.

Common and Proper Nouns

Underline each noun. Write *CN* above each common noun and *PN* above each proper noun.

> Example:
>
>   **PN**   **CN**   **CN**
>
> <u>Maria Tallchief</u> is the <u>daughter</u> of an Osage <u>father</u>
>
>   **CN**
>
> and a Scots-Irish <u>mother</u>.

1. Maria Tallchief was born in Fairfax, Oklahoma.

2. Her family moved to Los Angeles, California, where she began dance lessons.

3. Tallchief studied ballet with a famous teacher for five years and gave a performance at the Hollywood Bowl.

4. Tallchief left Los Angeles and auditioned in New York City, New York.

5. Tallchief married the famous choreographer George Balanchine and danced with the New York City Ballet.

6. She became a respected prima ballerina and was named Woman of the Year by President Eisenhower.

Plural Nouns

Write the plural form of each singular noun.

Rules for changing singular nouns to plural nouns:	
Most nouns add *-s* or *-es*.	bird**s** solo**s** dish**es** hero**es**
If a noun ends in a vowel plus *-y*, add *-s*.	chimney**s**
If a noun ends in a consonant plus *-y*, change the *-y* to *-i* and add *-es*.	penn**ies**
For some nouns ending in *-f*, add *-s*. For other nouns ending in *-f* or *-fe*, change the ending to *-v* and add *-es*.	chief**s** wol**ves**
Some plural nouns are spelled the same as the singular form. Some nouns are irregular and do not follow a rule.	deer mice men

	Singular	Plural		Singular	Plural
1.	lion	_____	2.	valley	_____
3.	dress	_____	4.	drum	_____
5.	copy	_____	6.	piano	_____
7.	bench	_____	8.	holiday	_____
9.	foot	_____	10.	belief	_____
11.	moose	_____	12.	leaf	_____

Possessive Nouns

Write the singular possessive, plural, and plural possessive form of each singular noun.

> To make a singular noun possessive, add 's.
> Example: the hamster**'s** wheel
>
> To make a plural noun that ends in -s possessive, add an apostrophe (') after the -s.
> Example: the girl**s'** dog
>
> To make a plural noun that does not end in -s possessive, add 's.
> Example: the children's cat

	Singular	Singular Possessive	Plural	Plural Possessive
1.	herbivore			
2.	video			
3.	cube			
4.	chef			
5.	penny			
6.	bus			
7.	class			
8.	hornet			
9.	dish			
10.	horse			

Personal Pronouns

Circle each personal pronoun.

A **pronoun** is a word that takes the place of a noun. A **personal pronoun** refers to a specific person, place, or thing. Personal pronouns include *I, me, we, us, he, him, she, her, it, they, them,* and *you.*

Example: (I) hope Riley remembers to give the letter to (her).

Personal pronouns can be possessive. **Possessive personal pronouns** include *mine, my, your, yours, her, hers, his, its, our, ours, their,* and *theirs.*

Example: The red and white coat is (mine).

1. Charlie could not find a jacket that he liked.

2. Bailey was excited to join us on our fishing trip.

3. Mr. Chou wanted me to solve the problem.

4. I was relieved to find his missing watch.

5. Ours is a very happy family of five.

6. Brad cannot believe that you found it!

7. We were surprised that Mrs. Bolla came to visit.

Indefinite and Demonstrative Pronouns

Underline each pronoun. Write *I* above each indefinite pronoun and *D* above each demonstrative pronoun.

An **indefinite pronoun** refers to a general person, place, or thing. Indefinite pronouns include *all, anybody, someone, either, few, neither, several, no one, nothing,* and *most.*

Example: <u>Someone</u> rang the doorbell and left a package. [I]

A **demonstrative pronoun** refers to a specific person, place, or thing. Demonstrative pronouns include *this, that, these,* and *those.*

Example: <u>That</u> is my favorite pair of jeans. [D]

1. Where will the electrician install that?

2. Why are these in the basket?

3. This is Dad's favorite dessert.

4. Most read Quinn's article and enjoyed it.

5. No one should say an unkind word.

6. Several have never been used before.

7. The class will make clay models with those.

8. Has anybody saved a favorite toy?

Action Verbs

Underline each action verb.

An **action verb** tells what a person, place, or thing is doing.
Example: Hurricane Katrina <u>damaged</u> much of the Louisiana coastline in 2005.

1. Hurricane Carla hit the Texas coast on September 10, 1961.

2. Hurricane Andrew struck Florida on August 24, 1992.

3. In 1965, Hurricane Betsy turned from Florida to Louisiana.

4. In 1969, Hurricane Camille created flooding in Virginia.

5. Camille brought winds up to 200 miles (320 km) per hour.

6. Hurricane Celia caused $1.6 billion in damage.

7. High winds demolished an airport.

8. Hurricane Gilbert made landfall in Jamaica.

Helping Verbs

Underline each helping verb.

Sometimes, an action verb is paired with a **helping verb**. The helping verb "helps" the action verb by telling things such as time and mood. Some common helping verbs include *am, are, had, has, have, is, shall, was, were,* and *will.*

                   helping verb   action verb

Example: The soccer game was enjoyed by the fans.

1.   The forward had dribbled the ball down the field.

2.   Jermaine, the goalie, was guarding the goal.

3.   The Racers team is trying hard to win.

4.   Their opponents, the Runners, are trying to defeat them.

5.   The Runners had scored easily the last time they played.

Write a helping verb to complete each sentence.

6.   I _____ singing in the chorus today.

7.   Marta _____ played the flute in last year's program.

8.   Who _____ play the piano in the recital tomorrow?

9.   Anthony _____ begun to play the violin.

Linking Verbs

Underline each linking verb.

A **linking verb** "links" the subject to the rest of the sentence. Linking verbs tell how things are, feel, or seem. Some common linking verbs include *am*, *appear*, *are*, *become*, *been*, *being*, *feel*, *is*, *look*, *seem*, *was*, and *were*.

                               linking verb

Example: My cousin is a firefighter.

1. Whales are fascinating animals.

2. Whales are mammals that breathe through one or two openings on top of the head.

3. The two major groups of whales are toothed whales and baleen whales.

4. I am interested in learning about what toothed whales eat.

5. A baleen whale's baleen plates look like sieves.

6. The baleen plate is helpful in straining food from seawater.

7. Blue whales are the largest baleen whale species.

8. The average length of a blue whale is 70 feet (21 m).

Simple Verb Tenses

Write _PR_ if the underlined verb or verbs are in the present tense, _PA_ if they are in the past tense, or _F_ if they are in the future tense.

The tense of a verb tells time. The three simple verb tenses are present, past, and future.

A **present-tense verb** tells what action is happening now.
Examples: We <u>type</u> our reports on the computer.
Ariel <u>is</u> a computer programmer.

A **past-tense verb** tells what action happened earlier.
Examples: Ashley <u>typed</u> her report on the computer.
Aaron <u>was</u> a computer programmer.

A **future-tense verb** tells what action will happen.
Examples: William <u>will type</u> his report on the computer.
Elaina <u>will be</u> a computer programmer.

1. _____ The tennis match <u>was postponed</u> because of rain.

2. _____ Last year's champion <u>will play</u> against her sister.

3. _____ The Canadian player <u>defeated</u> his opponent in three sets.

4. _____ This tennis match <u>is</u> very exciting to watch.

5. _____ The American <u>played</u> a difficult match against the Australian.

6. _____ The crowd <u>enjoys</u> the fast pace of the match.

7. _____ The Wimbledon Championships <u>will be</u> the next challenge.

Irregular Verbs

Circle the verb in parentheses that correctly completes each sentence.

An **irregular verb** does not form the past tense by adding -*d* or -*ed* to the present tense.

Irregular verbs in the past tense are usually spelled differently than their present-tense forms.

Common Irregular Verbs

Present	Past	Present	Past	Present	Past
become	became	go	went	sing	sang
begin	began	know	knew	take	took
bring	brought	eat	ate	write	wrote
give	gave	see	saw	tear	tore

1. Travis (went, gone) swimming earlier today.

2. We (freezed, froze) the food for longer storage.

3. The children (grew, grown) quickly this summer.

4. Elise (drived, drove) her sister to school on Monday.

5. The wind (shook, shaked) several apples from the trees.

6. The mayor (throwed, threw) the first pitch of the game.

7. I (took, taked) back the book to the library yesterday.

Review: Nouns, Pronouns, and Verbs

Write the letter of the correct part of speech from Column B to identify each underlined word or phrase. Some questions will have more than one answer.

Column A	Column B
1. _____ I <u>will find</u> the book.	A. possessive proper noun
2. _____ He <u>has studied</u>.	B. common noun
3. _____ Are <u>you</u> going?	C. proper noun
4. _____ This is <u>Ashley's</u> bicycle.	D. future-tense verb
5. _____ The man <u>was</u> a star.	E. linking verb
6. _____ Javier <u>talked</u> on the phone.	F. past-tense verb
7. _____ The storm <u>has</u> demolished the shed.	G. indefinite pronoun
8. _____ Can <u>anybody</u> help me?	H. action verb
9. _____ The <u>dog</u> ran home.	I. present-tense verb
10. _____ The <u>girls</u> who are singing are my cousins.	J. helping verb
11. _____ <u>Alice</u> saw Tom.	K. personal pronoun
12. _____ The computer <u>seems</u> fine now.	L. plural noun

Descriptive and Limiting Adjectives

Underline each adjective. Write _D_ above each descriptive adjective and _L_ above each limiting adjective.

An **adjective** modifies a noun or a pronoun. A **descriptive adjective** describes a noun and adds details about the noun. A **limiting adjective** tells quantity or number.

Examples: Laura wore a <u>yellow</u> coat.
    (D above yellow)

The <u>three</u> sisters went to <u>several</u> stores.
    (L above three and L above several)

1. Maria wants to buy a little silver sports car.

2. Many candidates filed their proposals on time.

3. Of the three runners, Clarke was the only one who finished.

4. Keisha is a great friend and a talented musician.

5. A few students have the flu.

6. Our closest neighbor has two gray cats and two black cats.

7. On Valentine's Day, Samantha received a dozen red roses.

8. Four little boys ate the green apples.

Demonstrative Adjectives

Underline each demonstrative adjective. Draw an arrow to the noun that it modifies.

A **demonstrative adjective** points out a specific person, place, or thing. Demonstrative adjectives include *this*, *that*, *these*, and *those*. The demonstrative adjective always comes before the noun it modifies.

Examples: That slice of watermelon was delicious.

Please put these green glasses on the shelf.

1. That storm is why I wanted you home early.

2. This nest has three eggs, and that nest has only two.

3. Will you help me put these plants in the garden?

4. Mrs. Lee lives in that beautiful yellow house on this street.

5. Did you put those trash cans at the curb?

6. This red apple is actually quite good.

7. Who are those people in the front row?

8. Did you see that car parked next to mine?

9. Those cherries growing on that tree look ripe.

Adjectives That Compare

Write the comparative and superlative form of each adjective. Some have been done for you.

A **comparative adjective** compares two nouns or pronouns. A **superlative adjective** compares three or more nouns or pronouns.

For most adjectives, add *-er* or *-est* to make the comparative and superlative forms.

For adjectives that end in a consonant preceded by a single vowel, double the final consonant and add *-er* or *-est*.

For adjectives that end in an *-e*, drop the *-e* and add *-er* or *-est*.

For adjectives that end in a *-y* preceded by a consonant, change the *-y* to *-i* and add *-er* or *-est*.

	Adjective	Comparative	Superlative
1.	new	newer	newest
2.	large	larger	largest
3.	easy	easier	easiest
4.	wet	wetter	wettest
5.	high		
6.	tall		
7.	fast		
8.	strong		
9.	hot		
10.	big		
11.	dry		
12.	fierce		
13.	funny		

Adjectives with *More* or *Most*

Write *more* or *most* before each underlined adjective to complete each sentence.

> Most adjectives that are three syllables or longer use *more* or *most* to compare people, places, and things. Some two-syllable adjectives also use *more* or *most*.
>
> Examples: The Grand Canyon at sunrise is **more** beautiful than I imagined.
>
> The Grand Canyon at sunrise is the **most** beautiful thing I have seen.

1.   The rocky trail was _____ dangerous than they remembered.

2.   *My Side of the Mountain* is the _____ interesting book we have read this year.

3.   That movie had the _____ terrible ending of any I have seen.

4.   His apology was _____ sincere today than yesterday.

5.   This is the _____ fragrant rose in the garden.

6.   Your card was the _____ thoughtful gift you could have given to me.

Adverbs

Write *YES* if the underlined word is an adverb. Write *NO* if the underlined word is not an adverb.

An **adverb** modifies a verb, an adjective, or another adverb. Most adverbs end in *-ly*, but some do not.

Examples:

V
Justin runs <u>daily</u> with the track team.

ADJ
<u>Very</u> cloudy skies were followed by heavy rain.

ADV
Janine answered <u>rather</u> quickly.

1. _____ The frog jumped <u>suddenly</u>.

2. _____ Josh <u>quickly</u> drank his juice.

3. _____ I wrote it on my <u>monthly</u> calendar.

4. _____ A parrot can <u>easily</u> imitate what she hears.

5. _____ Traffic was slow because of <u>early</u> morning fog.

6. _____ Who took this <u>unusual</u> photograph?

7. _____ The new neighbors seem <u>extremely</u> friendly.

8. _____ The <u>happy</u> dog greeted the school bus.

9. _____ Be sure to speak <u>clearly</u>.

10. _____ Would you like to hear a <u>silly</u> joke?

11. _____ The <u>startled</u> birds flew away.

12. _____ Her <u>deep</u> green glasses hid the color of her eyes.

Adverbs That Compare

Write the correct form of each adverb in parentheses.

> A **comparative adverb** compares two actions. A **superlative adverb** compares three or more actions.
>
> If an adverb has one syllable, add -er to make the comparative form and -est to make the superlative form.
>
> | fast | fast**er** | fast**est** |

1. Quiana runs (slow) _____ than Matthew.

2. That soccer team practices the (long) _____ of the three teams.

3. Jonathan works (hard) _____ than his brother.

4. Emily finished her homework (soon) _____ than Sarah.

5. The tuba sounds (low) _____ than the flute.

6. Who sang (loud) _____, Todd, Lisa, or Maria?

7. Is your house (near) _____ to the school than mine?

8. The sparrows flew (high) _____ than the robins.

9. Ramon dug the hole the (deep) _____ of his friends.

Adverbs with *More* or *Most*

Write *more* or *most* and the correct form of each adverb in parentheses to complete each sentence.

An adverb that ends in -*ly* or has more than one syllable uses *more* to make the comparative form and *most* to make the superlative form.

| quickly | **more** quickly | **most** quickly |

1. The blue team navigated the canoe (skillful) _____ than the green team.

2. The sea lions ate their lunch the (rapid)_____ of all of the ocean animals.

3. Shauna responded the (polite) _____ of her classmates.

4. The hummingbird flew (swift)_____ to the bird feeder than the swallow.

Write the comparative and superlative forms of each adverb.

	Adverb	Comparative	Superlative
5.	carefully		
6.	lazily		
7.	hungrily		
8.	joyously		

Irregular Adjectives and Adverbs

Fill in each blank with the comparative or superlative form of the word in parentheses. Some of them are irregular. Use a dictionary if you need help.

Irregular adjectives and irregular adverbs are spelled much differently to make comparative and superlative forms.

Common Irregular Adjectives and Adverbs	Comparative	Superlative
good/well	better	best
many	more	most
little	less	least
bad/badly	worse	worst

		Comparative	Superlative
1.	sing (badly)	sing _____	sing _____
2.	(many) trees	_____ trees	_____ trees
3.	(good) answer	_____ answer	_____ answer
4.	(clear) skies	_____ skies	_____ skies
5.	(bad) weather	_____ weather	_____ weather
6.	(little) rainfall	_____ rainfall	_____ rainfall
7.	feeling (well)	feeling _____	feeling _____

Review: Adjectives and Adverbs

Read each sentence carefully. Write *correct* if the sentence uses adjectives and adverbs correctly. Rewrite and correct the sentence if it uses adjectives and adverbs incorrectly.

1. Her greeting was more friendlier than his.

   _____

2. Eat moderate and you will lose weight.

   _____

3. Stephen is a lot confidenter now.

   _____

4. Whatever Elizabeth does, she does well.

   _____

5. I played the game as good as he did.

   _____

6. The entire menu looked good to us.

   _____

7. Michael is the most happiest child I know.

   _____

Prepositional Phrases

Underline each prepositional phrase. Circle each preposition. Sentences may have more than one prepositional phrase.

A **preposition** tells the relationship between two words in a sentence. Some prepositions include *about, above, across, after, around, before, behind, below, beside, except, for, from, in, near, of, off, on, out, over, through, to, under, up,* and *with.*

A **prepositional phrase** begins with a preposition and ends with a noun or pronoun. A prepositional phrase often tells where someone or something is, when something happens, or what something is like.

Example: The woman (in) the blue chair is my mother.

1. After the concert, we praised Daniel for his performance.

2. Olivia practices for one hour every day.

3. Benjamin has met all of his goals.

4. The students met by the pond in the park.

5. I saw that story yesterday in the newspaper.

6. When I talked with Morgan before the meeting, she agreed with me.

Prepositional Phrases

Add a prepositional phrase to each sentence.

1. The prince went into the forest _____ .

2. Susie and I are working together _____ .

3. _____ is where my cat likes to sleep.

4. The teacher calmly waited _____ .

5. Jennifer had never ice-skated _____ .

6. Toys were everywhere _____ .

7. I have read many books _____ .

8. The street _____ is Spring Street.

9. The 17th Street Bridge will be built _____ .

10. Our close friend _____ stayed two weeks.

11. The new red car _____ belongs to Joshua.

12. _____ , the flag flies on a high pole.

13. The firefighters battled the fire _____ .

Prepositional Phrases

Circle each prepositional phrase.

Growing a Sunflower

Did you know that you can plant a sunflower seed inside a cup? It is simple and fun! First, gather the following materials: a clear, plastic cup; a wet paper towel; and a sunflower seed. Next, place the paper towel in the cup. At this point, make sure that the paper towel covers the entire inside of the cup. Place the seed on the paper towel and fold the paper towel over the seed. Then, place the cup on a table near a window. Make sure that a lot of sunlight is shining through the window. If your plant does not get enough sunlight, it will not be able to grow. It will take three weeks for your seed to sprout. Meanwhile, record in a notebook any changes that you observe. Finally, you will be able to see your sunflower flourish!

Coordinating Conjunctions

Circle each coordinating conjunction. Write _W_ if the coordinating conjunction joins words, _P_ if it joins phrases, or _C_ if it joins clauses.

> A **conjunction** connects words or groups of words. A **coordinating conjunction** connects single words, phrases, and clauses. The most common coordinating conjunctions include _and, but, or,_ and _nor._
>
> Examples: __W__   Bring your lunch (and) money.
>
>   __P__   Your purse is on the couch (or) near the table.
>
>   __C__   Ava placed an ad in the newspaper, (but) no one responded.

1. _____ Matt pressed the button, and the engine started.

2. _____ Would you rather wash the dishes or dry them?

3. _____ Tony has three brothers and two sisters.

4. _____ Grace is going to the movie, but Luke is going shopping.

5. _____ Corinna plays soccer, volleyball, and softball.

6. _____ Christopher would never argue or complain.

7. _____ Look under the bed and in the closet.

8. _____ The little puppy was cute and active.

9. _____ Destini and Kara went camping, but I stayed home.

Correlative Conjunctions

Underline each pair of correlative conjunctions.

Correlative conjunctions connect items or word groups of the same kind. They are always used in pairs.

Common Correlative Conjunctions

either, or

both, and

neither, nor

not only, but also

whether, or

Examples: The work is <u>not only</u> profitable <u>but also</u> pleasant.

<u>Both</u> Hector <u>and</u> José are outstanding chess players.

1. Either we will buy the computer now, or we will wait for the next sale.

2. Gina both lifts weights and exercises.

3. Mrs. Clark will return your phone call whether she is here or away.

4. Neither my mother nor I was home this morning.

5. You can be sure that Seth will want either three or four slices of cheese.

6. Caleb will be not only faster but also less expensive than the lawn-care crew.

Subordinating Conjunctions

Underline each subordinating conjunction.

A **subordinating conjunction** begins an adverb clause. Subordinating conjunctions include *after, although, as, because, before, if, since, than, though, unless, until, when, whenever, where, wherever,* and *while.*

An **adverb clause** contains a subject and a verb but does not express a complete thought. An adverb clause tells relationship, such as time or cause and effect.

Example: It has not rained <u>since</u> last week.

1.   Because I finished my homework, I could watch my favorite show.

2.   Tell me when you are ready to leave.

3.   Before the day is over, I will finish my science project.

4.   Whenever it rains, the roof leaks.

5.   While you were out, your grandmother called.

6.   I will not do well unless I study hard.

7.   We will go to the movies after we eat dinner.

8.   Although the coach seemed strict, she was fair.

Review: Conjunctions

Underline each conjunction. Write *CO* if the conjunction is coordinating, *CR* if the conjunction is correlative, and *SUB* if the conjunction is subordinating.

1. _____ Either Felicia or Heath will decorate the cafeteria for the dance.

2. _____ Please bring crepe paper, tape, and poster board.

3. _____ Jack wanted to sing, but he had a sore throat.

4. _____ Until the dance is over, all students must remain in the cafeteria.

5. _____ Whenever the music stopped, all of the dancers changed partners.

6. _____ The dance was not only for fifth graders but also for sixth graders.

7. _____ Some students wanted country music but not rock music.

8. _____ As you know, Mrs. Drake was voted the best faculty dancer of the evening.

9. _____ The band will be paid whether or not we make a profit.

10. _____ After the dance was over, the cleanup committee stayed for hours.

Interjections

Underline each interjection.

> An **interjection** is a word or group of words that expresses an emotion. An exclamation point is used if the emotion is strong. An interjection that expresses less emotion often begins the sentence and is followed by a comma.
>
> Examples: Ouch! I twisted my ankle.
>
> Ah, that was a job well done.

1. Great! I got an A+ on my social studies project.

2. Oh no! You cannot write on the desk.

3. Can you believe how cold it is? Good grief!

4. Oh, what a beautiful sunset that is!

5. School is out for the summer. Hurray!

Write an interjection to begin each sentence.

6. _____! What a beautiful dress that is.

7. _____, you must be our new student.

8. _____! We are having a science test tomorrow.

9. _____! I spilled the water.

Review: Parts of Speech

Write the correct abbreviation for each underlined part of speech.

ADJ	adjective	INT	interjection	PRO	pronoun
ADV	adverb	N	noun	V	verb
CON	conjunction	PREP	preposition		

1. _____ The pink lemonade tasted very sour.

2. _____ From that angle, she can barely see my face.

3. _____ Jars of apples, pears, and peaches were on the shelves.

4. _____ My father leaned his ladder against the stone wall.

5. _____ The teacher asked the students to close their spelling books.

6. _____ Jimmy poured a bucket of water over the rose bushes.

7. _____ Yellowstone National Park is a popular tourist attraction.

8. _____ My grandmother said that the spaghetti was delicious.

9. _____ The sprinter ran so quickly that we could not believe our eyes.

10. _____ Uncle Henry gathered the ingredients before baking his casserole.

11. _____ Look out! Your back tire is almost flat.

Review: Parts of Speech

Identify the part of speech for the underlined word or words in each clue. Write the part of speech to solve the crossword puzzle. Some letters have been filled in for you.

Across

4. The cat's paw was sore.
6. Mya is a smart girl.
8. Ross was a good student.
9. The dog is in the house.

Down

1. Jackson has grown taller.
2. The teacher wrote carefully on the board.
3. Diego and Juan are my brothers.
7. Where are my shoes?

Simple Subjects

Underline each simple subject.

The **simple subject** is the main noun or pronoun that tells who or what a sentence is about.

Examples: The <u>bird</u> in the tree sang beautifully.
<u>They</u> ran to the park.
<u>Amy</u> drank her milk.

1. The heavy downpour lasted for several minutes.

2. The game of lacrosse has become very popular.

3. That square peg will not fit in this round hole.

4. Obviously, her slippers were too big for her.

5. The two dogs barked playfully at each other.

6. After a strong gust of wind, the man's hat landed in the mud.

7. The bucket of paint tipped over when the chair fell.

8. Two tubs of ice will be needed for the class picnic.

9. When we finally launched it, our new boat ran very well.

Simple Predicates

Underline each simple predicate.

The **simple predicate** is the main verb that tells what a subject is or does. The simple predicate may include one or more helping verbs and a main verb.

Examples: Shauna <u>ran</u> all the way home in the rain.

Shauna <u>is changing</u> her wet clothes.

1. The Johnsons painted their house recently.

2. Taylor is carrying a different backpack today.

3. Tornadoes have been seen in that area.

4. Trisha took a long trip last summer.

5. The oldest desks will be replaced.

6. George ran a few errands this morning.

7. The damage to the fence is being repaired.

8. Lisbon has one of the most beautiful ports in the world.

9. The wind has been blowing for several hours.

10. Originally, it was used as a residence by the royal family.

Compound Subjects

Underline each compound subject.

A **compound subject** contains two or more simple subjects. The simple subjects are joined by a conjunction, such as *and, or,* or *nor.*

Examples: <u>Zoe</u>, <u>Jill</u>, and <u>April</u> went to the movies.

<u>Nicholas</u> or <u>Victor</u> will make the morning announcements.

1. Dustin and Beth threw a surprise party for me.

2. My friends and family attended the party.

3. When the party was over, either Beth or Thomas cleaned the kitchen.

4. Eric and Donna offered me a ride home.

5. Later, my mother and father surprised me with another gift.

6. A necklace and bracelet were in the gift box.

7. Neither Aunt Jackie nor Uncle Bill could attend the party.

8. At noon, a card and gift arrived from my aunt and uncle.

9. A scarf and gloves were in the package.

Compound Predicates

Underline each compound predicate.

A **compound predicate** contains two or more simple verbs that have the same subject.

Example: Terrence <u>rides</u> the bus to school and <u>walks</u> home.

1. The students liked the speaker but disliked the homework.

2. Tristan and Sasha attended the play and drove home.

3. They listened to the band and enjoyed their songs.

4. When the concert ended, the audience applauded and chanted for more.

5. We ate the tacos and devoured the dessert.

6. After the ceremony ended, the children ran and played.

7. Tanner sings and dances in the school play.

8. Last night, Jessica studied, listened to music, and watched TV.

9. The driving instructor gave suggestions and asked questions.

Complete Subjects and Predicates

Underline each complete subject once. Underline each complete predicate twice.

A **complete subject** contains a simple subject and any other words that tell who or what the sentence is about. A **complete predicate** contains a simple predicate and any other words that describe the actions of the subject or the condition of the subject.

                   complete subject   **complete predicate**

Example: The red, juicy tomatoes were absolutely delicious.

1. My great-aunt loves to draw and paint landscapes.

2. The new, blue sports car was parked in the lower parking lot next to the old, green station wagon.

3. *Star Wars* is my favorite movie series of all time.

4. My friend Dawn and her little sister visited us yesterday.

5. Max and his father attended a professional football game last weekend.

6. My least favorite book was about a boy and his pet snake.

Independent Clauses

Underline each independent clause.

An **independent clause** expresses a complete thought and can stand alone as a sentence. A **dependent clause** does not express a complete thought and cannot stand alone. It must be connected to an independent clause.

independent clause

Examples: We can eat peanuts or raisins when we get hungry.

independent clause

If it is noon in Atlanta, what time is it in San Diego?

1. Although she was afraid of heights, Brooke joined the mountain-climbing club.

2. Mr. Rizzo climbed the ladder that was leaning against the tree.

3. I have been awake since the sun came up.

4. Dustin ate the cheese biscuit while he walked to school.

5. Brady decided to throw away his bubblegum, which lost its flavor.

6. The woman raked the leaves until she heard thunder in the distance.

Dependent Clauses

Underline each dependent clause. Circle the subordinating conjunction or relative pronoun that begins each dependent clause.

A dependent clause can begin with a subordinating conjunction (such as *although*, *if*, *since*, *because*, *when*, or *until*) or with a relative pronoun (such as *that*, *which*, or *who*).

dependent clause

Examples: Mario is a good student (because) he always tries his best.

1.   Jennie's parents looked for the toddler who was hiding under the dining room table.

2.   If you hear the doorbell, will you open the door for your grandmother?

3.   The vase, which was priceless, fell to the floor and shattered.

4.   We parked the car in the garage because it is raining.

5.   The music that Stan was playing was very relaxing.

6.   The wind was blowing gently as I fell asleep.

Clauses

Write an independent clause or a dependent clause to complete each sentence. Write *D* above each dependent clause.

> **D**
> Example: When he came home from school, Gabriel
> grabbed his skateboard.

1. If it does not rain today, _____
    _____

2. _____
    _____
    the doctor said to drink plenty of liquids.

3. Because Monday is a holiday, _____
    _____

4. The jacket _____
    was on sale last week.

5. My best friend, Serena, _____
    _____ also takes dance lessons.

6. Brenda is the fastest pitcher _____
    _____

Sentence Fragments

Write a complete sentence using each sentence fragment.

A **sentence fragment** is a group of words that does not express a complete thought and is not a complete sentence.

Examples: During my summer vacation (sentence fragment)
During my summer vacation, I learned how to scuba dive. (complete sentence)

1. completing my project _____

_____

_____

2. under the old apple tree _____

_____

_____

3. was my least favorite food _____

_____

_____

4. surrounded by the sharks _____

_____

_____

Subject-Verb Agreement

Circle the verb in parentheses that agrees with the subject in each sentence.

The verb of a sentence must agree with its subject. If the subject is singular, the verb must be singular. If the subject is plural, the verb must be plural.

Examples: A doctor (help, (helps)) people. She (cure, (cures)) aches.

Doctors ((help), helps) people. They ((cure), cures) aches.

1. He (live, lives) in the new house on Willow Street.

2. Some TV channels (show, shows) the funniest commercials.

3. You (need, needs) to study for your science test.

4. His sisters (play, plays) on the community soccer team.

5. The fifth-grade class (participate, participates) in the spelling bee.

6. Many people (enjoy, enjoys) the annual state fair.

7. My entire family (love, loves) camping in the mountains.

8. I (has, have) enjoyed meeting all of her friends.

Agreement with Phrases

Write the verb in parentheses that correctly completes each sentence.

Sometimes a prepositional phrase separates the subject from the verb. Read carefully to be sure that agreement is always between the verb and the subject of a sentence.

Examples: The <u>members of the garden club</u> **are planting** rose bushes in the square.

The **bird** <u>in the bushes</u> **sings** every morning.

1. (cause, causes) Insects on the corn_____ great damage to the crop.

2. (prove, proves) His experiment with electricity _____ the theory.

3. (show, shows) The scientists at Fernbank Science Center _____ their experiments to children.

4. (sell, sells) The new store in the mall _____ a variety of items.

5. (bark, barks) The puppy in her yard _____ at every passerby.

6. (respond, responds) The computers on each desk _____very rapidly.

Agreement with Plural Nouns

Write the verb in parentheses that correctly completes each sentence.

> A noun that ends in -s is not always plural and does not always agree with a plural verb.
>
> Examples: Thirty cents **was** the price of the candy.
>
>   Mumps **is** now a rare childhood disease.

1.   (slide, slides) The boy's glasses _____ down his nose.

2.   (has, have) Her running shorts _____ blue stripes down the sides.

3.   (is, are) Social studies _____ my favorite subject in school.

4.   (was, were) Door prizes_____ given at the annual banquet.

5.   (has, have) My pants _____ a hole in the knee.

6.   (appear, appears) The camera lens_____ to be broken.

7.   (cut, cuts) My scissors _____ more easily since they were sharpened.

Here, There, or Where

Write the correct form of *here's, there's, where's, here are, there are,* or *where are* to complete each sentence.

The contractions *here's* (here is), *there's* (there is), and *where's* (where is) are always singular and agree with singular nouns. *Here are, there are,* and *where are* agree with plural nouns.

Examples: **Here's** the dessert for dinner.

Here are the desserts for dinner.

1. _____ the peanut butter cookies that you and I baked?

2. _____ the book that you wanted.

3. _____ my green sweater?

4. _____ the moon, hiding behind a cloud.

5. _____ all of the assignments I promised.

6. _____ the wild horses, grazing on the plain.

7. _____ one more example of subject-verb agreement.

8. _____ the board games that you borrowed?

9. _____ the mountaintop that we plan to climb.

10. _____ your ticket for the show?

Subjects Joined by *Or* and *Nor*

Circle the verb in parentheses that correctly completes each sentence.

> Singular subjects joined by *or* or *nor* use a singular verb. If a singular and a plural subject are joined by *or* or *nor*, the verb should agree with the subject it is closest to.
>
> Examples: A peach or a strawberry <u>tastes</u> good with cereal.
>
> Whipped cream or marshmallows <u>are</u> good with hot chocolate.

1. Neither the blue jeans nor the sweatshirt (was, were) appropriate for the dance.

2. Both asparagus and turnip greens (taste, tastes) good to me.

3. Either Dylan or Valerie (has, have) seen the Web site about ancient Egypt.

4. The chocolate cake or the brownies (win, wins) the students' vote every time.

5. Neither Bob nor Virginia (need, needs) to write a special report.

6. Either the lemon or the orange spray (clean, cleans) best.

Agreement with Titles and Places

Circle the verb in parentheses that correctly completes each sentence.

> Company names, titles of publications, and names of specific places that end in -s agree with singular verbs, even if the title is plural in form.
>
> Examples: *Computer Updates* <u>is</u> my sister's favorite magazine.
>
> St. Louis, Missouri, <u>has</u> the famous Gateway Arch.

1. Texas (was, were) admitted to the Union in 1845.

2. The name *Texas* (come, comes) from the American Indian word *taysha*, which means "friends" or "allies."

3. Three Rivers (is, are) located in the southern Texas plains.

4. Each autumn, people of Scottish descent (gather, gathers) at Salado for a meeting and games.

5. *The Lone Star Times* (report, reports) the details of the annual event.

6. The German settlement of New Braunfels (celebrate, celebrates) the Sausage Festival each November.

7. "Texas, Our Texas" (is, are) the state song.

Agreement with Compound Subjects

Circle the verb in parentheses that correctly completes each sentence.

> Most sentences that contain a compound subject joined by *and* agree with the plural form of a verb. However, if the compound subject is treated as only one person, place, or thing, it agrees with a singular verb.
>
> Examples: The new sofa and chair <u>have arrived</u> today.
>
> Peanut butter and jelly <u>is</u> my favorite sandwich.

1. My computer and printer (has, have) been in the shop this week.

2. Ham and eggs (is, are) my grandmother's favorite breakfast.

3. Tara and Shannon (work, works) together well.

4. The wear and tear on my jeans (make, makes) them more comfortable.

5. Corned beef and cabbage (is, are) my sister's favorite dinner.

6. The pitcher and catcher (practice, practices) for four hours each day.

7. Homemade macaroni and cheese (taste, tastes) best.

Agreement with Indefinite Pronouns

Write an indefinite pronoun that agrees with each verb.

Some indefinite pronouns always agree with singular verbs.
These include *anybody, anyone, anything, each, either,*
everybody, everyone, everything, neither, nobody, no one,
nothing, one, someone, and *something.*

Some indefinite pronouns always agree with plural verbs.
These include *both, few, many, others,* and *several.*

Examples: <u>Anybody</u> **is** welcome to join the party.

   <u>Many</u> **have** already responded to the invitation.

1. _____ of my friends has taken karate.

2. _____ of the students have completed their
   projects.

3. _____ the coach or the principal knows the
   starting time of the game.

4. _____ is able to accomplish that task.

5. _____ of my parents enjoy bowling.

6. _____ has received an invitation to the
   wedding.

7. _____ of my classmates are going skiing this
   weekend.

8. _____ wants to miss the program on Friday.

Agreement with Indefinite Pronouns

Circle the verb in parentheses that correctly completes each sentence.

> Some indefinite pronouns, such as *all*, *any*, and *some*, can agree with either a singular or a plural verb. The verb form depends on the noun or pronoun that is referred to.
>
> Examples: Most of the salad <u>was</u> gone.
>
>   Most of us <u>were</u> tired.

1. All of the bread (was, were) eaten by the boys.

2. Most of those birds (migrate, migrates) in winter.

3. Most of the pizza (was, were) gone when I arrived home.

4. All of the children (swim, swims) in the neighborhood swimming pool.

5. Some of the games (is, are) more difficult than others.

6. Many of us (volunteer, volunteers) to take out the trash.

7. Any of her poems (is, are) enjoyable to read to the class.

8. Most of the teams (practice, practices) every day.

Review: Agreement

Underline the subject-verb agreement errors in the story. Write the correct word above each error. Can you find all 10 errors?

Katie and Beth was traveling to Australia for a summer tour. The magazines on the plane was helpful in making the long trip seem shorter. When they arrived at the airport in Sydney, everyone on the tour were most helpful in getting the luggage. Neither Katie nor Beth were too tired to take an evening tour of Sydney Harbor.

Katie and Beth soon learned that Australians loves outdoor sports because of the warm, sunny climate. Skin diving, surfing, swimming, and boating is some of the popular sports in Australia. Many Australians also plays golf and tennis.

The next day, Katie asked, "Where are the Great Barrier Reef?"

The guide responded, "We will have to travel farther north to see the reef."

Then Katie said, "Most people thinks that the Great Barrier Reef is all one reef, but it contains more than one reef."

"That's right, Katie. Some islands and reefs extends in a nearly unbroken chain for more than 1,000 miles (1,609.3 km) along the northeast coast," replied the guide.

Commas with Independent Clauses

Rewrite each sentence pair as one sentence joined by the conjunction in parentheses. Use a comma where needed.

A coordinating conjunction such as *and, or, nor*, or *but* joins two independent clauses and usually has a comma (,) written before it. However, if the two independent clauses are short and closely related, no comma is necessary.

Examples: Beverly made chicken salad**, and** Cynthia baked muffins.

The clouds disappeared **and** the sun shone.

1. Coco's puppies were brown and white. They were cute. (and)

   _____

   _____

2. Josh came to the meeting. He had to leave early. (but)

   _____

   _____

3. You can wash the dishes. You can take out the trash. (or)

   _____

   _____

Commas with Dependent Clauses

Underline each dependent clause. If the dependent clause begins the sentence, write a comma.

When a sentence begins with a dependent clause, a comma should appear before the independent clause. When a dependent clause follows the independent clause, no comma is needed.

Examples: Although clauds were forming, it had not begun to rain.

We wore boots because it started snowing.

1. When the weather changed I caught a bad cold.

2. I stayed indoors until the weather improved and my cold was gone.

3. If I go for a walk in the snow I think I will wear gloves.

4. Before I go I will make a list of the supplies we need.

5. The sky has become much darker although it is still early.

6. Because I plan to go to the movies my mother wants me to finish my chores early.

7. I feel proud whenever I think about my dog winning first place.

Commas with Phrases

Write commas where needed.

> When a sentence begins with one or more prepositional
> phrases, a comma separates the last one from the subject.
>
> Example: In some areas of the world, dolphins are abundant.

1. In length most dolphins are about six feet (two meters).

2. Off the coast of Japan scientists have identified about
    30,000 to 50,000 white-sided dolphins.

3. Above the upper jaw a dolphin has a mass of fat and tissue
    that looks like a bulging forehead.

4. In short bursts dolphins can reach speeds of 23 to 25 miles
    (37 to 40 km) per hour.

5. In the bow wave of a moving ship observers often see
    dolphins swimming.

6. By using the thrust of the ship dolphins can actually ride the
    wave.

7. About every two minutes dolphins come to the surface to
    breathe.

Commas with Interrupters

Punctuate each sentence correctly.

An expression that interrupts a sentence is set apart with commas. **Interrupters** include words used as direct address, appositives, and parenthetical expressions.

Examples: Janelle, what is your question? (direct address)
Alvin, a gardener, raked the leaves. (appositive)
This movie, obviously, is very boring. (Parenthetical Expression)

1. André please take out the trash before you go to play basketball.

2. The science project on electricity in my opinion should win first prize.

3. Before you leave empty the dishwasher and put away the dishes Kimberly.

4. Tia my distant cousin has arrived for a week's visit.

5. Jessi will of course win the spelling bee this year.

6. Read this science fiction book Jason and tell me your opinion.

7. Did you hear Gabriela the new student sing in the audition?

Colons and Commas in a Series

Write a comma or colon where needed.

A colon should appear before a list of items, especially after the phrase *the following*.

Example: Please bring to class the following: some paper, a pencil, your textbook, and a calculator.

A comma should appear after each item in a series, except the last item.

Example: Ask Danielle, Jamie, and Anna to help you.

1.   We drove through Texas Arizona and New Mexico.

2.   They used firm ripe unspotted bananas for the centerpiece.

3.   My supplies for the trip will include the following comic books puzzle books snacks and a game.

4.   The soup contained several healthy ingredients beans tomatoes peas carrots and pasta.

5.   This is the biggest ugliest dirtiest most lovable dog I have ever seen!

6.   He plans to buy the following items that will be on sale next week ice skates skis snowshoes ski pants and gloves.

Ending Punctuation

Write the correct ending punctuation for each sentence.

A period (.) is used at the end of a declarative or imperative sentence. A **declarative sentence** makes a statement, and an **imperative sentence** gives a command.

Examples: The old cat lay sleeping on the bed. (declarative)

Please open this can of corn. (imperative)

A question mark (?) is used at the end of an **interrogative sentence**. An interrogative sentence asks a question.

Example: Where are my brown boots?

An exclamation point (!) is used at the end of an **exclamatory sentence**. An exclamatory sentence expresses emotion.

Example: Look how fast the snow is falling!

1. Did you know that gold was discovered in California in 1848

2. It was the greatest gold rush in United States history

3. Can you believe that San Francisco, California, grew from a small town to a city of 25,000 people in one year

4. Use that large pick to mine for gold

5. Look at this huge gold nugget

6. The discovery of gold attracted thousands of prospectors

Quotation Marks

Rewrite each sentence. Write ending punctuation marks and quotation marks where needed.

Quotation marks (" ") are used before and after the exact words of a speaker. A comma or question mark separates the spoken words from the rest of the sentence and is placed inside the quotation marks.

Examples: "What are your plans for today?" Mrs. Conti asked.

Joey replied, "I am going to the park with friends."

Some quotations may be divided. Commas separate the quoted words from the rest of the sentence.

Example: "May I go with you," asked Jane, "or do you want me to ride with Dad?"

1.   Would you like to go to the park Ryan asked

_____

_____

2.   Are we going skating asked Timothy or swimming

_____

_____

3.   Ryan answered I would rather go skating today

_____

_____

Direct and Indirect Quotations

Write commas, quotation marks, and ending punctuation marks in each sentence where needed.

A **direct quotation** is a person's exact words. It begins with an uppercase letter and is set apart from the rest of a sentence by quotation marks and commas.

Example: Jennifer said, "Be sure to eat your vegetables."

An **indirect quotation** does not use quotation marks. It is not the exact words of the person speaking.

Example: Jennifer reminded me to eat my vegetables.

1.   Patrick asked Where are my new tennis shoes

2.   I think I saw them under your bed replied Justin

3.   Becky told me to look in my closet

4.   Nassim said My new shoes look the same as yours

5.   Lin wished that I would find them soon

6.   Kim suggested Can you wear your old ones today instead

7.   I found them yelled Becky from the living room

8.   Lin said that they were beneath the sofa

Titles

Rewrite each sentence using correct punctuation and capitalization.

The first word and the last word of a title and any important words in the title are capitalized. In most cases, the words *a, an, and, or, and the,* and most prepositions are not capitalized.

Underline:	Use quotation marks around:
• book titles	• titles of articles in books or magazines
• magazine titles	• chapter titles
• newspaper titles	• essay titles
• play and musical titles	• short story titles
• movie titles	• song titles
• TV show titles	• poem titles

Examples: <u>Walking in the Waves</u> is an amazing book.

If you whistle "Summer Song," the dog will howl with you.

1. We watch get a grip every Saturday night at 8:00.

    _____

2. I borrowed Sasha's favorite book, the moon news.

    _____

3. Logan memorized the poem june bug for his presentation.

    _____

4. Carla just read the broken arm, so she has two chapters left.

    _____

Capitalization

Underline each word that should begin with a capital letter.

Always capitalize:
- the first word in a sentence
- the first word in a direct quotation
- proper nouns
- initials
- the pronoun *I*
- proper adjectives

1. mrs. hernandez said, "i enjoy playing with my dog, coco."

2. juanita told her parents that her spanish teacher was from south america.

3. juanita said, "i am going to argentina with my friends kristen and olivia."

4. we want to visit buenos aires and iguazu falls while we are there.

5. when we return, mrs. locklear, our social studies teacher, wants us to talk about our trip to argentina.

6. "i can hardly wait to leave," said olivia.

Capitalization

Underline each word that should begin with a capital letter.

> ### Always capitalize:
> - days of the week
> - names of continents, countries, states, and cities
> - names of geographic features, such as rivers, mountains, and oceans
> - months of the year
> - abbreviations of proper nouns

1. the rocky mountains in utah is my favorite vacation spot.

2. on thursday, august 27, the powell family reunion will be held at blue lake park in oklahoma city, oklahoma.

3. "will you attend the rockin' robins concert at rigby arena in atlanta, georgia, on saturday, february 3?" asked alan.

4. "no, i will not be able to attend the concert because i will be in seattle, washington," replied dante.

5. the st. lawrence river in canada flows about 800 miles (1,300 km) from lake ontario to the gulf of st. lawrence.

6. the white cliffs of dover in the united kingdom are visible on a clear day by the people of calais, france.

Direct and Indirect Objects

Write *V* above each verb, *DO* above each direct object, and *IO* above each indirect object. Some sentences may not have an indirect object.

A **direct object** is a noun or pronoun that receives the action of a verb. An **indirect object** is a noun or pronoun that tells to whom or for whom the action is done. To have an object, the verb must be an action verb. If a sentence has an indirect object, it must have a direct object.

Examples:

$$\overset{V}{The\ policeman\ showed}\ \overset{DO}{his\ badge.}$$

$$\overset{V}{The\ policeman\ showed}\ \overset{IO}{the\ man}\ \overset{DO}{his\ badge.}$$

1. The police officers directed traffic.

2. Officer Samson gave one man a warning.

3. The speeders told the officers their excuses.

4. Officer Johnson read some drivers their rights.

5. Many people attended the trial.

6. The judge raised her gavel.

Interrogative and Relative Pronouns

Write *I* above each underlined interrogative pronoun and *R* above each underlined relative pronoun. If the pronoun is relative, circle the dependent clause.

An **interrogative pronoun** asks a question. Interrogative pronouns include *who, whom, which, what,* and *whose.*
A **relative pronoun** introduces a dependent clause in a sentence. Relative pronouns include *who, whom, whose, which, that, whichever, whatever, whomever,* and *whoever.*

Examples:
$\overset{I}{\underline{Who}}$ is going to the dance?

$\overset{R}{\text{The boy}}\underline{(who\ is\ dancing)}$ is my brother.

1. For <u>whom</u> did you decide to vote?

2. <u>Who</u> will win the election?

3. Rembrandt is the artist <u>whom</u> I am studying.

4. You may choose <u>whomever</u> you want to help you.

5. The photographs <u>that</u> Diana asked to see are in the album.

6. For <u>whom</u> is the party being given?

7. The toddler cannot tell us <u>what</u> he wants.

Contractions

Circle the contraction in parentheses that correctly completes each sentence.

A **contraction** is a word that combines two words. One type of contraction combines a verb and *not*. Another type of contraction combines a pronoun and a verb. An apostrophe (') tells where letters have been left out. The verb in a contraction must agree with the subject of the sentence.

Examples: We <u>aren't</u> having volleyball practice today.

<u>She'll</u> go to the store for us.

1. Mother said that it (wasn't, weren't) time for dinner.

2. (Where's, Where are) my gloves and hat?

3. (Don't, Doesn't) worry about the test tomorrow.

4. (Here's, Here are) proof that the dog ate the cupcake.

5. The airline (doesn't, don't) serve food on this flight.

6. (There's, There are) rain in the forecast for tomorrow.

7. The boys (isn't, aren't) making the movie today.

8. Jan and Leah (wasn't, weren't) ready to give their report.

9. Valerie (hasn't, haven't) skated since third grade.

Double Negatives

Circle the word in parentheses that correctly completes each sentence.

A sentence may contain the word *no* or words that mean *no*. A word that means *no* is a **negative**. Negatives include *no*, *nobody*, *no one*, *nothing*, *none*, *nowhere*, and *never*. The word *not* and contractions made with *not* are also negatives. A **double negative** is an error caused by using two negatives together in a sentence.

Incorrect	Correct
I **don't** have **nothing** for homework tonight.	I **don't** have **anything** for homework tonight.
We're **not** going **nowhere** this summer for vacation.	We're **not** going **anywhere** this summer for vacation.

1. Isabella wasn't (ever, never) going to doubt her brother.

2. Clarke didn't go (nowhere, anywhere) without his comb.

3. We don't want (any, no) pizza for lunch today.

4. Wouldn't (nobody, anybody) help you with your chores?

5. (Weren't, Were) none of you going shopping at the mall?

6. I can't find (anything, nothing) to wear to the party.

Double Comparisons

Circle the word or words in parentheses that correctly completes each sentence.

> An adjective or adverb in the comparative form ends in -er or -est, or it begins with *more, most, less,* or *least.* A **double comparison** is an error caused by using both comparative forms together.
>
> Examples: This kite is constructed **more better** than any other kite in the sky.
>
> This kite is constructed **better** than any other kite in the sky.

1. Donna read the (thickest, most thickest) book in the library.

2. This sweater is (more handsomer, more handsome) than that one.

3. Jake is the (happiest, most happiest) puppy I know.

4. Kevin's car is the (fastest, most fastest) one on the track.

5. This handwriting is the (most awfulest, most awful) of all.

6. Mina's essay was the (least shortest, shortest) in the contest.

7. Our garden looks (better, more better) since I watered it.

8. The clown was the (funniest, most funniest) performer.

Homophones

Circle the word in parentheses that correctly completes each sentence.

Homophones are words that are pronounced the same but have different meanings and spellings.

Common Homophones

your belonging to you	to in the direction of	there in that place	peak the highest part
you're you are	**too** also	**they're** they are	**peek** to glance at
	two the number 2	**their** belonging to them	

1. Where are (your, you're) (to, two, too) copies of the report?

2. (Their, They're, There) sitting behind the desk.

3. I did not (peek, peak) at my surprise present.

4. I will meet you (their, they're, there).

5. I think that (your, you're) going to receive an A on this.

6. The hikers wanted (to, two, too) reach the mountain's (peak, peek).

Synonyms and Antonyms

Circle the synonym or synonyms for each word. Use a thesaurus or a dictionary if you need help.

Synonyms are words that have similar meanings. **Antonyms** are words that have opposite meanings.

Example: big

Synonyms	Antonyms
large	little
huge	tiny
gigantic	small

1. **walk:**   stroll   skip   run

2. **funny:**   comical   mad   sad

3. **mad:**   angry   cross   irate

Write _A_ for antonyms or _S_ for synonyms to describe each pair of underlined words.

4. _____ The dog was <u>large</u>, and the cat was <u>small</u>.

5. _____ The <u>empty</u> sky was <u>void</u> of clouds.

6. _____ The <u>poisonous</u> plant seemed <u>harmless</u> at first.

Goofy Grammar 1

Complete this activity with friends or on your own. First, write a word for each part of speech. Next, fill in the blanks on page 72 using the words you chose. Then, read the completed story aloud. Have fun!

1. plural noun (place) _____

2. action verb _____

3. plural noun _____

4. noun (a sound) _____

5. plural noun _____

6. plural noun _____

7. adjective _____

8. plural noun _____

9. action verb _____

10. comparative adjective _____

11. adjective _____

Goofy Grammar 1:
"The Truth about Crickets"

Crickets sometimes invade people's _____
                                                    1
and become pests by their presence. Homeowners complain that

crickets continuously _____ , especially at night.
                                2
While indoors, crickets feed on a wide variety of things, such as

fabrics, _____ , and even other crickets.
                    3

The name *cricket* comes from the high-pitched

_____ that crickets make. This
                    4
sound is produced when the male cricket rubs its front

_____ together to attract a female. You can
                    5
identify different kinds of crickets by listening to their songs.

Crickets resemble long-horned _____ .
                                            6
Adult house crickets are almost 1 inch (2.5 cm) long and are

_____ . They have three _____
            7   8
on their heads. The wings of the cricket _____
                                                        9
on the side of their bodies.

Ground crickets are much _____ . They have
                                        10
long spines on their hind legs. However, their songs are often

_____.
        11

Goofy Grammar 2

Complete this activity with friends or on your own. First, write a word for each part of speech. Next, fill in the blanks on page 74 using the words you chose. Then, read the completed story aloud. Have fun!

1. common noun _____

2. common noun _____

3. plural proper noun _____

4. common noun _____

5. action verb _____

6. proper noun _____

7. action verb _____

8. action verb _____

9. adverb _____

10. action verb (ending in *-ing*) _____

11. past-tense verb _____

12. comparative adjective _____

Goofy Grammar 2: "The Brothers"

Once upon a _____ there were three
                               1

brothers named Thomas, Samuel, and Wayne. These three were

very close and did everything together. They even played on the

same _____ team. The team was called the
                        2

_____ .
        3

Thomas was the _____ on the team. His job
                          4

was to _____ . This was very important because
         5

the team was in first place in the _____ League.
                                    6

Samuel's job on the team was to _____ .
                                     7

This allowed the team to be able to _____
                                    8

_____ . He was the number one person in the
        9

league at this position.

Wayne was the captain of the team. He was always

_____ to help his team win. The more he
        10

_____ the _____ the team
        11   12

became.

Answer Key

Page 3
1. CN = gerbil, mammal, hamster;
2. CN = species, gerbil; PN = Asia, Africa; 3. CN = Gerbils, enemies;
4. CN = gerbil, legs, birds, predators;
5. CN = Gerbils, stores, descendants, gerbils, decades; PN = Mongolia;
6. CN = gerbil, food, bottle;
PN = Christopher, Pet Town;
7. CN = gerbil, home, brother, sister;
PN = Christopher, Shane, Sierra;
8. CN = family, gerbil, pet

Page 4
1. Maria Tallchief, PN; Fairfax, PN; Oklahoma, PN; 2. family, CN; Los Angeles, PN; California, PN; lessons, CN; 3. Tallchief, PN; ballet, CN; teacher, CN; years, CN; performance, CN; Hollywood Bowl, PN; 4. Tallchief, PN; Los Angeles, PN; New York City, PN; New York, PN; 5. Tallchief, PN; choreographer, CN; George Balanchine, PN; New York City Ballet, PN; 6. ballerina, CN; Woman of the Year, PN; President Eisenhower, PN

Page 5
1. lions; 2. valleys; 3. dresses;
4. drums; 5. copies; 6. pianos;
7. benches; 8. holidays; 9. feet;
10. beliefs; 11. moose; 12. leaves

Page 6
1. herbivore's, herbivores, herbivores'; 2. video's, videos, videos'; 3. cube's, cubes, cubes';
4. chef's, chefs, chefs'; 5. penny's, pennies, pennies'; 6. bus's, buses, buses'; 7. class's, classes, classes';
8. hornet's, hornets, hornets';
9. dish's, dishes, dishes'; 10. horse's, horses, horses'

Page 7
1. he; 2. us, our; 3. me; 4. I, his;
5. Ours; 6. you, it; 7. We

Page 8
1. that, D; 2. these, D; 3. This, D;
4. Most, I; 5. No one, I; 6. Several, I;
7. those, D; 8. anybody, I

Page 9
1. hit; 2. struck; 3. turned; 4. created;
5. brought; 6. caused; 7. demolished;
8. made

Page 10
1. had; 2. was; 3. is; 4. are; 5. had;
6. am; 7. had; 8. will; 9. has

Page 11
1. are; 2. are; 3. are; 4. am; 5. look;
6. is; 7. are; 8. is

Page 12
1. PA; 2. F; 3. PA; 4. PR; 5. PA; 6. PR;
7. F

Page 13
1. went; 2. froze; 3. grew; 4. drove;
5. shook; 6. threw; 7. took

Page 14
1. D, H; 2. F, H; 3. K; 4. A; 5. E, F; 6. F, H; 7. J; 8. G; 9. B; 10. B, L; 11. C; 12. E, I

Page 15
1. little, D; silver, D; sports, D; 2. Many, L; 3. three, L; only, L; 4. great, D; talented, D; 5. few, L; 6. closest, D; two, L; gray, D; two, L; black, D;
7. dozen, L; red, D; 8. Four, L; little, D; green, D

Page 16
1. that→storm; 2. This→nest; that→nest; 3. these→plants;
4. that→house; this→street;
5. those→cans; 6. This→apple;
7. those→people; 8. that→car;
9. Those→cherries; that→tree

Page 17

5. higher, highest; 6. taller, tallest;
7. faster, fastest; 8. stronger,
strongest; 9. hotter, hottest;
10. bigger, biggest; 11. drier, driest;
12. fiercer, fiercest; 13. funnier,
funniest

Page 18

1. more; 2. most; 3. most; 4. more;
5. most; 6. most

Page 19

1. YES; 2. YES; 3. NO; 4. YES; 5. NO;
6. NO; 7. YES; 8. NO; 9. YES; 10. NO;
11. NO; 12. YES

Page 20

1. slower; 2. longest; 3. harder;
4. sooner; 5. lower; 6. loudest;
7. nearer; 8. higher; 9. deepest

Page 21

1. more skillfully; 2. most rapidly;
3. most politely; 4. more swiftly;
5. more carefully, most carefully;
6. more lazily, most lazily; 7. more
hungrily, most hungrily; 8. more
joyously, most joyously

Page 22

1. worse, worst; 2. more, most;
3. better, best; 4. clearer, clearest;
5. worse, worst; 6. less, least;
7. better, best

Page 23

1. Her greeting was friendlier than
his.; 2. Eat moderately and you will
lose weight.; 3. Stephen is a lot
more confident now.; 4. correct; 5. I
played the game as well as he did.;
6. correct; 7. Michael is the happiest
child I know.

Page 24

1. After the concert, for his
performance; 2. for one hour; 3. of
his goals; 4. by the pond, in the park;
5. in the newspaper; 6. with Morgan,
before the meeting, with me

Page 25

1.–13. Answers will vary.

Page 26

Circle the following phrases: inside a
cup; in the cup; inside of the cup; on
the paper towel; over the seed; on
a table; near a window; through the
window; in a notebook

Page 27

1. C, and; 2. P, or; 3. W, and; 4. C,
but; 5. W, and; 6. W, or; 7. P, and;
8. W, and; 9. W, and; C, but

Page 28

1. Either, or; 2. both, and; 3. whether,
or; 4. Neither, nor; 5. either, or;
6. not only, but also

Page 29

1. Because; 2. when; 3. Before;
4. Whenever; 5. While; 6. unless;
7. after; 8. Although

Page 30

1. Either, CR; or, CR; 2. and, CO;
3. but, CO; 4. Until, SUB;
5. Whenever, SUB; 6. not only, CR;
but also, CR; 7. but, CO; 8. As, SUB;
9. whether or not, CR; 10. After, SUB

Page 31

1. Great!; 2. Oh no!; 3. Good grief!;
4. Oh,; 5. Hurray!; 6.–9. Answers will
vary.

Page 32

1. V; 2. PRO; 3. CON; 4. PREP;
5. ADJ; 6. PREP; 7. ADJ; 8. N; 9. ADV;
10. V; 11. INT

Page 33

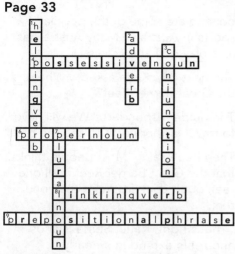

Crossword:
- 1 down: helpingverb
- 2 down: adverb
- 3 down: conjunction
- 4 across: possessivenoun
- 5 down: pluralnoun
- 6 across: propernoun
- 8 across: linkingverb
- 9 across: prepositionalphrase

Page 34
1. downpour; 2. game; 3. peg;
4. slippers; 5. dogs; 6. hat; 7. bucket;
8. tubs; 9. boat

Page 35
1. painted; 2. is carrying; 3. have
been seen; 4. took; 5. will be
replaced; 6. ran; 7. is being repaired;
8. has; 9. has been blowing; 10. was
used

Page 36
1. Dustin, Beth; 2. friends, family;
3. Beth, Thomas; 4. Eric, Donna;
5. mother, father; 6. necklace,
bracelet; 7. Aunt Jackie, Uncle Bill;
8. card, gift; 9. scarf, gloves

Page 37
1. liked, disliked; 2. attended, drove;
3. listened, enjoyed; 4. applauded,
chanted; 5. ate, devoured; 6. ran,
played; 7. sings, dances; 8. studied,
listened, watched; 9. gave, asked

Page 38
1. My great-aunt loves to draw and
paint landscapes.; 2. The new, blue
sports car was parked in the lower
parking lot next to the old, green
station wagon.; 3. *Star Wars* is my
favorite movie series of all time.;
4. My friend Dawn and her little sister
visited us yesterday.; 5. Max and
his father attended a professional
football game last weekend.; 6. My
least favorite book was about a boy
and his pet snake.

Page 39
1. Brooke joined the mountain-
climbing club; 2. Mr. Rizzo climbed
the ladder; 3. I have been awake;
4. Dustin ate the cheese biscuit;
5. Brady decided to throw away his
bubblegum; 6. The woman raked the
leaves

Page 40
1. who was hiding under the dining
room table; 2. If you hear the
doorbell; 3. which was priceless;
4. because it is raining; 5. that Stan
was playing; 6. as I fell asleep

Page 41
1.–6. Answers will vary.; 1. If it
does not rain today = D; 2. (new
part of sentence) = D; 3. Because
Monday is a holiday = D; 4. (new
part of sentence) = D; 5. (new part
of sentence) = D; 6. (new part of
sentence) = D

Page 42
1.–4. Answers will vary.

Page 43
1. lives; 2. show; 3. need; 4. play;
5. participates; 6. enjoy; 7. loves;
8. have

Page 44
1. cause; 2. proves; 3. show; 4. sells;
5. barks; 6. respond

Page 45
1. slide; 2. have; 3. is; 4. were;
5. have; 6. appears; 7. cut

Page 46
1. Where are; 2. Here's or There's;
3. Where's; 4. There's; 5. Here are or
There are; 6. There are; 7. Here's or
There's; 8. Where are; 9. There's;
10. Where's

Page 47
1. was; 2. taste; 3. has; 4. win;
5. needs; 6. cleans

Page 48
1. was; 2. comes; 3. is; 4. gather;
5. reports; 6. celebrates; 7. is

Page 49
1. have; 2. is; 3. work; 4. makes; 5. is;
6. practice; 7. tastes

Page 50
Answers will vary but may include:
1. Each; 2. Few; 3. Either; 4. Anyone;
5. Both; 6. Everyone; 7. Several;
8. Nobody

Page 51
1. was; 2. migrate; 3. was; 4. swim;
5. are; 6. volunteer; 7. are; 8. practice

Page 52
Katie and Beth were traveling to
Australia for a summer tour. The
magazines on the plane were helpful
in making the long trip seem shorter.
When they arrived at the airport in
Sydney, everyone on the tour was
most helpful in getting the luggage.
Neither Katie nor Beth was too tired to
take an evening tour of Sydney Harbor.

Katie and Beth soon learned that
Australians love outdoor sports
because of the warm, sunny climate.
Skin diving, surfing, swimming, and
boating are some of the popular
sports in Australia. Many Australians
also play golf and tennis.

The next day, Katie asked, "Where is
the Great Barrier Reef?"

The guide responded, "We will have
to travel farther north to see the reef."

Then Katie said, "Most people think
that the Great Barrier Reef is all one
reef, but it contains more than one
reef."

"That's right, Katie. Some islands
and reefs extend in a nearly
unbroken chain for more than
1,000 miles (1,609.3 km) along the
northeast coast," replied the guide.

Page 53
1. Coco's puppies were brown and
white, and they were cute.;
2. Josh came to the meeting, but he
had to leave early.; 3. You can wash
the dishes, or you can take out the
trash.

Page 54
1. When the weather changed,;
2. until the weather improved and my
cold was gone; 3. If I go for a walk in
the snow,; 4. Before I go,; 5. although
it is still early; 6. Because I plan to go
to the movies,; 7. whenever I think
about my dog winning first place

Page 55

1. In length, most dolphins are about six feet (two meters).; 2. Off the coast of Japan, scientists have identified about 30,000 to 50,000 white-sided dolphins.; 3. Above the upper jaw, a dolphin has a mass of fat and tissue that looks like a bulging forehead.; 4. In short bursts, dolphins can reach speeds of 23 to 25 miles (37 to 40 km) per hour.; 5. In the bow wave of a moving ship, observers often see dolphins swimming.; 6. By using the thrust of the ship, dolphins can actually ride the wave.; 7. About every two minutes, dolphins come to the surface to breathe.

Page 56

1. André, please take out the trash before you go to play basketball.; 2. The science project on electricity, in my opinion, should win first prize.; 3. Before you leave, empty the dishwasher and put away the dishes, Kimberly.; 4. Tia, my distant cousin, has arrived for a week's visit.; 5. Jessi will, of course, win the spelling bee this year.; 6. Read this science fiction book, Jason, and tell me your opinion.; 7. Did you hear Gabriela, the new student, sing in the audition?

Page 57

1. We drove through Texas, Arizona, and New Mexico.; 2. They used firm, ripe, unspotted bananas for the centerpiece.; 3. My supplies for the trip will include the following: comic books, puzzle books, snacks, and a game.; 4. The soup contained several healthy ingredients: beans, tomatoes, peas, carrots, and pasta.; 5. This is the biggest, ugliest, dirtiest, most lovable dog I have ever seen!; 6. He plans to buy the following items that will be on sale next week: ice skates, skis, snowshoes, ski pants, and gloves.

Page 58

1. Did you know that gold was discovered in California in 1848?; 2. It was the greatest gold rush in United States history.; 3. Can you believe that San Francisco, California, grew from a small town to a city of 25,000 people in one year?; 4. Use that large pick to mine for gold.; 5. Look at this huge gold nugget!; 6. The discovery of gold attracted thousands of prospectors.

Page 59

1. "Would you like to go to the park?" Ryan asked.; 2. "Are we going skating," asked Timothy, "or swimming?"; 3. Ryan answered, "I would rather go skating today."

Page 60

1. Patrick asked, "Where are my new tennis shoes?"; 2. "I think I saw them under your bed," replied Justin.; 3. Becky told me to look in my closet.; 4. Nassim said, "My new shoes look the same as yours."; 5. Lin wished that I would find them soon.; 6. Kim suggested, "Can you wear your old ones today instead?"; 7. "I found them!" yelled Becky from the living room.; 8. Lin said that they were beneath the sofa.

Page 61

1. Get a Grip; 2. The Moon News; 3. "June Bug"; 4. "The Broken Arm"

Page 62

1. Mrs. Hernandez, I, Coco; 2. Juanita, Spanish, South America; 3. Juanita, I, Argentina, Kristen, Olivia; 4. We, Buenos Aires, Iguazu Falls; 5. When, Mrs. Locklear, Argentina; 6. I, Olivia

Page 63

1. The Rocky Mountains, Utah; 2. On Thursday, August, Powell, Blue Lake Park, Oklahoma City, Oklahoma; 3. Will, Rockin' Robins, Rigby Arena, Atlanta, Georgia, Saturday, February, Alan; 4. No, I, I, Seattle, Washington, Dante; 5. The, St. Lawrence River, Canada, Lake Ontario, Gulf, St. Lawrence; 6. The, White Cliffs, Dover, United Kingdom, Calais, France

Page 64

1. directed = V; traffic = DO; 2. gave = V; man = IO; warning = DO; 3. told = V; officers = IO, excuses = DO; 4. read = V; drivers = IO, rights = DO; 5. attended = V; trial = DO; 6. raised = V; gavel = DO

Page 65

1. I; 2. I; 3. R, whom I am studying; 4. R, whomever you want to help you; 5. R, that Diana asked to see; 6. I; 7. R, what he wants

Page 66

1. wasn't; 2. Where are; 3. Don't; 4. Here's; 5. doesn't; 6. There's; 7. aren't; 8. weren't; 9. hasn't

Page 67

1. ever; 2. anywhere; 3. any; 4. anybody; 5. Were; 6. anything

Page 68

1. thickest; 2. more handsome; 3. happiest; 4. fastest; 5. most awful; 6. shortest; 7. better; 8. funniest

Page 69

1. your, two; 2. They're; 3. peek; 4. there; 5. you're; 6. to, peak

Page 70

1. stroll; 2. comical; 3. angry, cross, irate; 4. A; 5. S; 6. A

Page 71

Answers will vary.

Page 72

Answers will vary.

Page 73

Answers will vary.

Page 74

Answers will vary.